Seeking the Pink

Seeking the Pink

Poems by

Liana Kapelke-Dale

Cover design by Shay Culligan

Cover Art by Liana Kapelke-Dale

ISBN: 978-1-63980-018-6

Kelsay Books
502 South 1040 East, A-119
American Fork, Utah 84003
Kelsaybooks.com

for my mother

and for A.D.,
who inspired many of these poems
whether he knows it or not

Acknowledgments

Big Easy Review: "young so young and in full Technicolor"

Blue Bonnet Review and *UW Flash Fiction:* "when we fell from the moon"

Duende Literary Journal: "Some Things Are More Delicate than Others"

The Fabulist: "Lead into Gold"

Fleas on the Dog: "Post-Modern Papyrus," "Pagophobic Logophobe," "saltwater taffy"

Grand Little Things: "Feral Love Song"

Impossible Task: "Total Blitz of the Heart"

Contents

If hot red is for anger and rage, pink is the color of a soft burning—hot enough to light up the dark corners of sadness and grief, but cool enough to be tender, innocent, open.

—Ibi Zoboi

I believe in pink. I believe that laughing is the best calorie burner. I believe in kissing, kissing a lot. I believe in being strong when everything seems to be going wrong. I believe that tomorrow is another day and I believe in miracles.

—Audrey Hepburn

Seeking the Pink

I think they will find, one day
long after my threadbare death,
that my bones are a fragile shade of pink.
Pale, as though they'd been run through
the laundry with a single red sock.

Pink tendrils twine hesitantly outwards
from my body, seek filaments
of golden jacquard and soft cotton
      stained crimson from lip rouge or blood
      or maybe both
to weave themselves into a wayward textile.
The strands are like
connective tissue between muscles, maybe.
They leave tails of light like
the neural pathways that
take me from sunbeams slipping
through windows onto worn-out rugs
to trails of milkweed seeds
floating on the brisk breeze in fall.

But the strands, finding no others,
retreat back inside my body,
wet with a colorless rain,
and twist tightly around my bones
as the pink seeps, deeper and deeper.

Ode to the Pear

Not *quite* ripe.
Still firm and fresh
as a young girl's breasts,
nipples still unsuckled.

Still crisp and almost crunchy,
as though apples grew in the tropics,
infused with a humid sweetness
with a bite less sharp than
northern apple's bark.

Still mellowly green,
not yet faded like when
slow summer fades to fleeting fall,
not yet juicy or succulent or
informed or full-figured
enough to make my taste buds
burn yellow blood-orange with
untimely flavor that seems like
it filled out too soon.

It must have.
The rawly sweet sugarcane fruit,
deceptively innocent in its demeanor,
ripened while I slept last night.

I want both.

The chaste and unseasoned pear,
gently grainy on my tongue,
tightly wound and tasting of
island balmy freshness, and

the ripened womb,
soft and curvy, overflowing
with sagacious juices
that run in sappy rivulets
down my chin and neck
and pass through
sticky cleavage.

I want both.

Practical Feminism with Lilith and Eve

I. The Great Unpeeling

I have an apple to peel with you, Eve.
Stole it from that serpent's tree
    while he was dozing.

Naughty girl!
You've become lithe as a cat
    burglar since you learned to climb trees.
But why did you only get one? Shouldn't we offer it to Adam first?

…You know, I've always preferred the Spanish *Adán,* actually
    an Adam is bound to be clean-shaven
        (I mean, just look at yours, sweeting),
    but an Adán grows scruff
        that could scratch a vexing itch
        even on the hottest summer day…
Ow! Okay, Eve. Sorry.
Hmm. Good question.
We *could* offer it to Adam first, of course,
    but you know how men are, lovely.
Women are much more open
    to trying new things
    and he'll just get all annoyed if it's not any good.
In any case, Adam's jerking off again
    over in that sunny glen by the koi pond.
    No, not that one,
    the one with all the fractal sunbeams
    and monarch butterflies—

Lilith! Don't *point!*

Anyway—shall we peel this apple?

16

II. Lilith Reflects

One loooooong, curlycued strip
     of sweet red peel
     twirling downwards in the breeze
         like the rocking of a rickety old spiral staircase
         the ripples of a dancer's swirling skirts
         the smooth shifting of a kaleidoscope
         the phases of the moon as it disappears
             bite by bite, like an apple to its core
             and grows again from planted seed to
ripened fruit
     its image glues to my brain
         with brush and paste
         like a page of propaganda
             smeared onto the wall
             of a hall of justice
         until it's swept away with a mop
             sopping in red paint

Then with a   **POP**
     like the sound of a big flash bulb

         my world is green again
         the apple skin,
         just skin

I peer at the peel
curly as the wound twine
     of cat's cradle
rosy red as soft untouched nipples

Maybe I'm crazy, but
the more apples I eat
the more I
     WANT
     to eat

It's not hard to be sly here
in the guise of a guileless girl
     in this garden
     that similarly seems
     without guile

The serpent is clever
     and as honorable
     as an early ancestor
     on the Machiavelli family tree can be,
         to be sure

He can hardly have failed to notice
how apples grow freely now
     sweeter with every crunch
and plentiful, if you know where to look

and I'd bet he's not happy
he no longer corners the market

There are new colors and shades among the fruit
every day
     musky pink ladies
     sour green grannies

They grow and I learn
as every branch leads to untasted flavors
new young apple blossoms, each
        struggling to ripen
        from a hypothesis into a theory

My sister Eve took a bite
        wide-eyed with the North Star
        above her
Eve used to feel warm and purposeful
when told the story of how a god
made her from Adam's rib

But now she can't shake the feeling
that she is all marrow
        made from the purest concentration
        of bone that protects Adam's heart
Eve's eyes peer out at me
from somewhere between
newly-formed dreadlocks
and a pair of serviceable Birkenstocks
        that she found while dumpster diving
She's still trying to find herself

And the serpent
sent Curiosity to kill the cat
burglar
but when he saw me next, I was
        stretched out nude
        on a crumbling terra cotta roof softened by evergreen flora
        purring so hard the loose rocks and shingles rumbled
            just a little

I flexed my claws lazily in the sun
       while Curiosity watched me in awe,
       rubbing my feet

Some Things Are More Delicate than Others

Some things are more delicate
than others.

Soft fingers link daisies into chains,
and my wounds are patched
with cobwebs and moss. In the garden,
rabbits feast on tulip buds while
I ponder the softness of fur
caught against the coarseness
of a trapper's calloused hand.

No one is innocent.

Loss is delicate.
The strands of connective tissue
that bound us together
separate, untying our lax hearts,
spiced like cinnamon bark and stained
with the ink of so many unwritten verses.

No one is culpable.

Rain tumbles down through the sky
like you and I once stumbled through
shameless bliss in my now empty bed.

Some things are more delicate
than others, easily torn between
careless fingers.

Skeleton

Shaking, my fleshless hands break
open the succulent.
Stripped of skin, clumsy bones
crush the plant to gelatin,
try to smooth cool aloe
onto the jagged, misshapen edges
of my empty ribcage
as they would onto a hot pink sunburn.
Deprived of muscle
and its denizen memory,
hands forget they were ever whole.

The weather is fickle.
I pack my chest cavity full with sandbags
to hold off flooding
when the rains come.
The sand is gritty and some spills,
settling into the alcoves
behind my kneecaps.

The rain washes it all away,
rinsing the granules in a waterfall
that races down my polished
tibiae and fibulae
till nothing remains.

Then the sun rises above me
and I cannot bear the heavy light
that shines down onto my shoulder blades.
It leaves me feeling bleached and sterile
as only a skeleton can.

But I wiggle my feet slowly in the day
and sense a soft moss growing between
the phalanges that were once my toes.

I have no eyes to perceive its color,
but somehow I see a bright spring
green spreading throughout
the crooks and crannies of my joints
and thriving in the secret spaces
once open only for me.

Holiest of Carbon-Based Life Forms

We are atomic warriors,
guarding a microscopic
Great Wall of China
from planetary monsters,
waiting to be plundered
by their next movement
across space.

We are the holiest
of carbon-based
life forms.

We codify the stars,
scribbling light from
ancient pens, transcribing
the laws of the universe
onto a yellow legal pad.

Watch us burn alive
on street corners
in protest of
cryonic love,

enamored with our own
organic ending.

Slaying the Dragon

i

Slay the dragon.

Pull the scythe
out from beneath the bed.

It's midnight; time
to embark on your quest.

ii

You're so afraid.

At the witching hour,
magical things happen.

The moon speaks in her silvertongued voice,
and an owl takes flight from your windowsill
as you dream:

> *Hekate,*
> *take me back to the shadow realm,*
> *where the girl who named me lives.*
> *I left her there.*
> *Take me back so I can save her.*
> *Please. Please. Please.*
> *Let me save her.*

A part of you resists the pull
of night.
You know you will be dragged down
into its depths,
lunatic.

You are so afraid.

> *Hekate, leave me to my fear.*
> *Let me save myself.*

iii

Failure is certain.

The dragon will drive one of its tail spikes
through your heart
and then it will roast you on a spit,
your eyes open but unseeing,
its fiery breath cooking you to a fine crisp
as it waits to strip and eat your flesh.

This time, the quest will kill you.

Quiver in terror.

Only one small timid rivulet
of hope still flows in your veins,
not nearly enough to quench your fear.

Scared you will quash it completely,
it whispers:

    …maybe the dragon will be small.

    Maybe you will have to walk the entire earth
    to find it, but when you do,
    maybe it will fit in the palm of your hand.

    Maybe the dragon will burn your hand,
    but the burns can be covered by band-aids.

    Maybe its teeth are no larger than needles.

    Maybe its tail is soft, rather than spiked.

    What if you leave your scythe
    under the bed,
    rather than carrying it
    the length of the planet,

    and when you find your dragon,
    what if you don't slay it?

What if you tame it
and let it sleep in the nest of your hair,
watching over your dreams?

    What if, instead of slaying the dragon,
    you let it save you instead?

matters of consequence

I know a certain red-faced gentleman. He has never loved anyone. And all day he says over and over, just like you: "I am busy with matters of consequence!"

—Antoine de Saint Exupéry

as i walk up the front steps
through summer's honeycombed

afternoon light
la vie en jaune

that washes everything over
with warm yellows

authentic sunbeams
through which we all must pass

two monarch butterflies
flirt with the breeze

their mating dance
fumbled and ecstatic

like origami, they bend and fold themselves toward
each other over and again over

as they try to stay in synch
against the air's current

but what chance have two such slight creatures
they tumble apart

and the untroubled wind continues along
off to deal with matters of consequence

Absent Orgasm

The pharmaceutical companies call
my inability to come
        "absent orgasm."

The phrase implies that my orgasm
is in a current state of existence,

but it's off galivanting elsewhere
at the moment.

So when I get asked that obnoxious question—
        "Did you finish?"—
with its oblivious querant and obvious answer,

now I can say,

"Unfortunately, my orgasm is currently absent."

From the Deathbed of a Perfume Historian

*It is...like a dream come true, or rather a tapestry of dreams. It is an attempt
to conquer time and death by recreating the past.*
  —Perfume expert Chant Wagner on the re-creation of Trianon, worn
    by Marie Antoinette

Hidden base notes
of tuberose and orange blossom
rise up through
crisp, ripe overtones—
a garden bed spilling over
with gardenias,
an orchard so lush
it covers the sky
with pears and apples—

like the gentle opening piano chords
of *Clair de Lune*
or the first drops of rain
that splash onto earth, before the rest
come rushing down.

If I could, I'd have bottled
the scent of petrichor,
a fresh transparency
with hints of grass and iron
like newly-mown lawn
over clay.

I'd have worn it on my skin
and in my hair—
the earthy aftermath
of a summer thunderstorm,
sweet against a light layer
of salty sweat on my epidermis.

That would have been a perfume
worth wearing.

But I never wore any scent myself.

It would have confused my nose,
which was my secret weapon,

my ace in the hole
that guided me to the top
of my trade.

Following my nose, I'd sense
hints to unanswered riddles,
inklings of jasmine or vanilla
that stood out from the fragrance,
subtle but clear
to my refined palette.

I've recovered and replenished
empty perfume bottles owned by
Marie Antoinette,
Mata Hari,
Madame Curie.
I reconstructed their aromas
until they were whole again.

The notes, individually
skeletal and harmless, together
merge into symphonic bliss
with the power to strike mute
any pompous king,

turn the most ardent patriots
into double agents,
discover radioactive love
amid nuclear waste.

I've spent my life
re-creating forgotten scents,
reviving the ghosts
of singular women
who live now
only on the wrists and clavicles
of any pedestrian who will pay.

I'd never have guessed
that I would regret the absence
of a fragrant creation of my own,

that I would regret
never attempting a distillation of
summer twilight,
blooming wisteria and lilac
just before they fade into dusk.

I could have made a liquid
that restored lost memories
and coaxed decisive caresses
from the uncertain.

But, though my legacy may be
mere reclamation,
still I caught a whiff of immortality
amidst the tuberose

as I preserved it
in a clear glass bottle.

Total Blitz of the Heart

with thanks to singer Bonnie Tyler

every now and then
a banshee hijacks my lungs then
screams
through my opened mouth
she can't
make it stop

lightning war

staccato. Sparks.
dissonant bombs Fall
in lonely Cminor
bowing to Beethoven

a sweet german shepherd named Stuka
I N M E M O R I A M
of.
Dive Bombers everywhere
Never Forget

Xrays shrouded in soot
no image available
broken bone as unseen as broken heart
please try again later
at a less cloudy date

stealth in the Dark

purring prowlers outside broken windows
bleeding onto shattered glass

Pain.

                                                You.

                                  depress a Flare
                                  into my sternum
                                        and Fire
                                       an S.O.S.
                              to signal my distress
                                 You hold me safe
                                try to seal the wound
                               with a righteous Kiss

                                          i fall apart

in my dark bunker

dumped here as suddenly
as an Atom bomb
as quickly
as nuclear Waste

blind in the darkness
beneath me i feel
a large wooden crate
i slit my fingers
between its planks

inside
packed with straw
something cold and Metal waits

                              35

as i touch it
steel shoots quickly
up and into my arm

    (Achtung!)

Compliments of Herr Mauser

    Danke, Mein Herr
    (du dreckiger Bastard)

The Gewehr 98
gets Loaded
with stripper clips
    (natürlich)

then Locks some lead
into my empty chest cavity

replaces with Live ammunition
another heart
lost in the Blitzkrieg

Freshwater meets salt.
As river kisses ocean,
Its mouth opens wide.

young so young and in full Technicolor

as the storks continue to fly
        dropping
           eggs down chimneys
i watch a close friend coo coo
and nuzzle her newborn
        whose shell cracked open
        just two weeks ago

she sends me photos of a milk-drunk
little creature with dark eyes

and i feel purple-blue clouds cry
milky raindrops above me
liquid freshwater pearls that bless me
with unrequited love

when finally i sleep
i find myself in a black-and-white world
        entering a club
        skipping the line
        walking past the bouncer
           who lifts the velvet rope for me
when i see David Bowie
        young so young
        and in full Technicolor
leather jacket red hair diamond eyes
somehow still waiting to be let in

i walk over to him
        feline-cool as ever
as he leans patiently against a pole
smoking a fag

and immediately i'm milk-drunk
       that smile those eyes that skin
       so many colors to imbibe
       so many diamonds to worship

we speak
       and the smile never leaves his face
       and not one hair out of place

and i'm not quite sure how it happens
but i ask him (terribly gauche)
       to give me his sperm

with his beautiful peaceful knowing smile still in place
and still in line for the concert
he hands me his *sample*
       which he just happens to have on him

our hands touch and i look down at them
feeling peachy-keenly his gift

one last rare smile and i'm ushered into the club
guarding his semen with my very life

fuck the band (whoever they are)
i run to the bathroom
       slaphappy-smooth and yet trembling with disbelief
open the container
to see his sperm
       young so young
       and in full Technicolor

bright cherry-blossom pink

Shangri La

i pass into an unseen world
when i think about you

a sweet Shangri La

settled deep
in a hidden valley

where the streets
i wander
barefoot in the rain

are cobbled pink brick

and the city's walls
that keep me safe inside
       as my heart gently squeezes
       safe inside my chest

are covered in peeling pink paint

warm mists envelop me
curling my hair
deepening my dimples
       as i think of your laugh

i close my eyes
in anticipation of
your long-awaited arrival

while outside
the snow stings

and caps the mountains
of Kunlun

Cheshire Cats and Lab Mice

Two nights ago, the moon waned
     almost completely
save for one remaining sliver,

a surprising gold
like a delicate gilded saucer or
the last thin slice of an orange rind or
the Cheshire Cat's grin in the seconds
before he fades completely from sight.

You want to ask his grin a question,
but the Cheshire is too elusive
to be pinned down to one
logical answer.

The Cat's smile mocks you,
knowing you cannot catch him,
knowing how badly you want to.

You tell yourself
you approach questions too rationally,
that you must relinquish control over the answers,

because when you ask a magic cat
a question, there will rarely
be just one correct response.

You try to tap into intuition
but the tap has dried up

and you are left in white sterility
with your bland, friendly lab mice.

You hurry to protect them, feed them, love them.
You force yourself to believe they are enough—
      they will provide all the answers you need.

You gild their cages and squeaky wheels
      that go nowhere,
offer up sweetened clementine rind as a special treat,
convince yourself you never saw a moon-cat's
wide orange-slivered grin

because Cheshire Cats exist only
in children's books
and words, once written,
have a tendency to remain on the page
      (you tell yourself).

Time goes by and you almost forget
the waning moon
and all the orange-colored treasures
it offered.

> *Come choose, the moon told you,*
>   *some amber or a tiger's eye*
>   *mewling ginger kittens*
>   *or a tree of crystallized tangerines.*
> *Take anything you wish to accompany you*
> *while I begin, again, to wax.*
> *Remember the ebb and flow of the tides.*

But instead you chose an empty white path
where musings and fantasies
could be cleaved away
until no unknowns remained.

You thought you and the mice would be safe there—

until one evening you wake
from a cat nap
and all your tiny companions
are gone.

You run to their broken gilded cages,
aghast with terrible understanding.

It turns out that Cheshire Cats
can walk off the page.

It turns out that every last little thing
can be cleaved away,
if claws are sharp enough.

It turns out that grief
in the dark of the moon
can still surprise you.

Pagophobic Logophobe

pagophobic (*adj.*):
(1)   of, pertaining to, or exhibiting pagophobia, the fear of ice and/or frost.
logophobe (*noun*):
(1)   one who suffers from logophobia, the fear of words and/or talking.

I'm frightened
Little tremors fumble through
my gut's firmament

I'm so afraid of my words   they might
slice downwards
like icicles
tear through paper

I can almost feel cold diamond shards
on my skin

Sometimes my words just

           drip

           so simply

           onto paper

           as though from

           paint

           at the tip

           of a brush

           or

water from

the eternal

faucet

and I invite breath deeply into my lungs

But now my words are dry frozen daggers
hypnotizing with their wry scintillating points
and my breath freezes as well   sharply

                                        below them

My fear is
of the potential to inflict
          mortal wounds
Winter's starry-eyed blades
could crackle down
onto unsuspecting heads
at any moment

and I am afraid

I cower   with   head in hands
back bowed
spine paralyzed into submission

                    We learned about this in elementary school
                              In case of: earthquake
                                        tornado
                                        blizzard
                                        flood

hurricane
nuclear war
etc.
please cover head with hands
because you can live without your hands
but not without your head

nor without your words

Feet sunk deep in snow
I stand below
looking up at sparkling translucence

    that could stab to the core

But I reach up
gently tug at the largest
               most deadly
icicle
until it breaks off cleanly
at the root

Sheathed in my hand
the icicle shines cold
frozen ripples distorting its clarity

The blood that blushes my skin begins
to soften the ice against my palm

and as I smile
at the thought
that the remaining icicles
are simply water paralyzed
clinging to a drainpipe
     like a kitten to a tree branch

the lethal weapon
melts in my hand

when we fell from the moon

last night i dreamt we fell from the moon
pulled downwards by earth's gravity

our hands curled tightly together
yours were locks and my fingers
the only keys that could open them

we hurtled silently toward the great circular blue
like divers into a deep yawning ocean
that had waited an eternity to embrace us

but when we finally hit the atmosphere
our bodies combusted in blue flame
breaking into particles of dust

the white flakes that were once
solid bone and resilient flesh

floated down to earth like snow
collecting on the ground
as though it were christmas morning

and the moon smiled at the sight of children
making angels that did not melt

depiction of adam and eve in pink

rose gold lipstick stains
my lips like
thin gold foil
covers pink petals

i want to smear
the rosy golden paint
all over someone's shirt collar

with one touch
of a fragile pink finger,
i'll trace rosy gold flowers on his skin,
raise pink gooseflesh,
begin already the ending

all parts of me are pink

pink flesh stretched over bone
pink beneath my nails
pink when my body turns
          inside out

a naïve color

a newborn color

like the ephemeral innocence
of adam and eve

pale pink
before
eve deflowered them both

adam,
that staid and stoic protector
of virtue,
cast away lilith
for lying beneath the devil
(her hardsoft crimson lover),
but becomes party to female crime
when he lies beneath eve
while she plucks his innocence
as she would a simple rosebud
(and it is over all too quickly)

so says the bible

in the rosy afterglow
(rosier for adam)
he shyly admits to eve
that he was never that into lilith, anyway
eve shrugs, eyes closed and unconcerned

she'd known since the first sweet crunch of apple
that man protects only the virtue
of those he does not want

separated from her by eons,
one thousand doctrinal male lies, and
possibly a dimension or two,

my greatest desire
is still to splinter male virtue

eve's hand is eager,
her fingers outstretched

51

with a fleshy appetite to know more,
she reaches out
from beneath the shade
of the apocryphal tree of knowledge

grasping adam's palm,
she brings her boy toy with her
to the new world

they will have proof of life known
stored inside their skulls
their pink brains coiled like serpents

in the glare of the sun
their skin tans,
eventually wrinkles

when he's cut
he bleeds crimson

and looks to her,
uncertain if she will bind
his wound

Junk Drawers and Purple Diamonds

My heart is not in a cage,
or a kennel,
or a tent.
It's not in a two-bedroom suburban house.
It's not in a caravan,
or a shack,
and it's certainly not in a mansion.

My heart is not out under the stars.
It is not beneath my skin.

My heart is hiding.
It is in a junk drawer,
full of worry about getting splinters
from the poorly-finished wood grain.

The junk drawer is filled
with the most tangible and useless
of objects:
  used batteries
  old phone chargers
  rubber bands
  dead flashlights.
My heart tells itself,
these things are life.
These things exist.

      Long ago, before the fear settled in,
    my heart flew as I played Capture-the-Flag
        with new friends in the dark.
      It ran with us through the corridors
         of my high school at night.

My heart was wise.
My skin was just skin
and my heart lived beneath it
and yes, everything was jumbled
like a junk drawer in the kitchen
but the drawer was open
and I could rifle through it,
raw and tender
and careful

but not too careful.

Now, it is inhibited.
It is all rind, no orange.
It cannot be peeled.

The thesaurus says that "anathema"
        is an antonym
        for love.

My heart is told that its love *is* anathema.
        But how can love *be* anathema?

My heart is buried by these words.
It feels safe beneath them,
certain I will be unable to dig it out.

Come out, heart, come out!

Your love is not soap opera.
It can be believed.

Your love is the kind of love
that happens in real life.

Your love is able to believe
in the unseen world.

Once, long ago,
I let myself believe.
I felt the connective tissue grow
between my own heart and a friend's.
One evening, we clasped hands
closed our eyes,
and I held an image firmly in my mind
willed it to travel from my body to hers.

And her eyes opened
and she said,

"purple diamond."

And my heart and I believed.

saltwater taffy

whenever i learn something new
about you
i tuck the information away
        in my wallet or jacket pockets
to salivate over

later

in the sanctity of my bedroom
i'll secretly take it out

like a sweet juicy piece
of saltwater taffy
that demands my attention

it challenges my dry mouth
not to water

i unwrap it
with surgical precision
not wanting to leave even the tiniest
sliver of candy
behind on the waxed paper

unable to wait any longer
i place the delicious morsel
        onto my tongue
close my eyes
and focus

on what i can taste
in this new flavor

A Ghazal at Night

Sensuous visions come to me at night.
What comes to you on this black silk-cat night?

Cat paws on the roof echoed my heart's beat.
The rain made my voice sound silken that night.

I deserve flowers only in the dark,
So a moonflower garden grows at night.

Butterflies and bees pollinate Morning
Glories in light—but the dark is bat's night.

You walk the garden path and watch for me.
The time is not ripe yet on this flat night.

I walk with bare feet, my soles against soil.
Flowers sprout behind, this (pitter-pat) night.

We grow in our garden by the same roots,
Thoughts together-apart chit-chat at night.

Skin-to-earth, but I dream of skin-to-skin—
You aren't here, this hot-thermostat night.

Morning Glory, moonflower, fern, and vine;
Our roots deep in soil every black-matte night.

We'll swing from lianas some young, bright day,
Til then, we will garden in that long night.

Lead into Gold

The ennui sets in
insidiously. A blue haze
creeps over the horizon
that marks the edge
of the kingdom.
Every time I look
out the window, I notice
that it has spread
a little bit more:
through the village,
up towards the castle.
It's come for me,
the sleepy tedium
that turns sizzling bliss
into leaden boredom.

Every morning I wake up
next to a prince—
the man who rescued me
from a life of servitude
and taught me to
be vulnerable as
crocus shoots in spring.
He petted my hardened frame
until the dried layers
peeled back willingly
to reveal a pale greenness.
He told me the stars
burned white-hot for us,
together, alone.
He promised me,
not just the stars,
but the whole expansive sky.

58

He loves me, I know,
and I him,
but it is never enough.
The stars are dimmed
by his lonely passion,
and guilt dissolves
my insides into
dark, cavernous pools.
Making love has become
rote, as bitter as eating
lotus roots.

At night, my dreams
carry me to a witch
dressed in red
who promises me nothing.
My hair tangles and snags
at her fingers' touch,
as she pulls my head back
to kiss my lips,
drawing blood with her teeth.
Come dawn I wake
with bruises scattered
about my body,
fresh and sore
but freely received.
Somehow, the prince
never notices these marks,
even as he roams the body
he believes to be his,
wholly.

But everything tempts me
now. The footmen,
who must avert their gaze
when they pass me, present
an engaging challenge.
When one inadvertently meets
my eyes, I lick my lips,
red like roses in the gardens
that bloom lush for just one day.
The men look startled,
but only for a moment.
After all, I'm the poster girl
for decorous love.
No one would believe
that I flirt with the servants
while wishing
that my fairy tale was never written.

Maybe someday,
I'll run away with the serving girl,
teach her to strip back
her layers until the green
beneath is bared.
I'll forget falling through
the sky's domain,
just to be caught in a web
of black lace veils.
I'll remember only
the charming man
who tried to extract me
from the agony of uncertainty
and the torment of loneliness,

not knowing that
two people can be
more alone, together,
than one, separate.

And I'll stay with the serving girl
until she leaves me,
or I leave her,
for a knife thrower in a traveling circus
or an alchemist
who has learned to transform
lead into gold.

Lemonade mélange

There she was. Like disco lemonade, yeah there she was.
—Marcy Playground, "Sex & Candy"

Maybe disco lemonade is what you drink to stay hydrated while on
the dance floor
Maybe it gives you a buzz, but is actually solid-gold non-alcoholic
refreshment
Like how rose-infused lemonade attracts bumblebees, as you drink
it in the heat of a Moroccan summer afternoon
Like how lemonade-stand lemonade is still sold on the corner for a
quarter
Like how your mama brought you cayenne lemonade as you
lounged by the bayou with your skinny, dirty-legged friends
Like how old folks drink mint lemonade in Floridian retirement
homes, thirstily downing the liquid before they lazily crush the
mint behind their ears

Rose lemonade is a perfume
Lemonade-stand lemonade is a fifty-cent memory of a day when
only two cars drove by
Cayenne lemonade is a satisfying sneeze straight into swampy
water
Mint lemonade is a palette-cleansing neck-cooler
Beyoncé's *Lemonade* is an album of juicy truths that burn yellow,
squeezed into our wounds
And disco lemonade, maybe, is a song that swirls off your tongue
while you watch your lover walk towards you under the mirrorball

Echo Speaks

In the beginning
Before Zeus wanted me
Before Hera cursed me
Before Narcissus spurned me

I was sound

I see Narcissus and I fall

     Or maybe I dive
     I can't be certain

He wastes away
     Cursed for his vanity
         —Such a small sin—
     And able to love only himself

If I were a swan
     I would swim to him
         I would send ripples over his reflection
            I would break the spell
        Nemesis has killed us both
     Broken on her divine Wheel

I would save him
And he would read the words I cannot speak
In my eyes as I look at him

I would tend to our inflamed hearts
     With witch hazel
     As I kiss his swollen mouth

But

I am only an Echo

And all he will ever hear from me
Are phantoms of the words that first bloomed in his own mouth

But in the beginning

I was sound

Feral Love Song

I want to howl mad on the moors for you,
To bay fiercely as lightning splits the sky
Hearing your laugh, knowing you see me true.

Though in the light we never can be two
(Sun and moon hear me and smile wry);
I want to howl mad on the moors for you.

The blitz of war in my head always knew
I would blow any fuse that I passed by—
Hearing your laugh, knowing you see me true.

You humble me; the flames I've sparked in you
Would burn my clothes and naked I would fly—
I want to howl mad on the moors for you.

I think of this when dreams turn salty-blue.
Without a thought, my heart is yours to try,
Hearing your laugh, knowing you see me true.

And with the dawn, I know your grasses grew;
Come dusk, you'll want to hear my feral cry.
I want to howl mad on the moors for you,
Hearing your laugh, knowing you see me true.

My Thief

why do i desire sleep
only when the sun is bright and jaunty

why do i fear darkness

why do i resist melting
into the arms of night

why do i grapple doggedly
with daydreams

grasp at them
clasp them to me

why do i abuse their sweetness
wringing it out of them

like i wring my hands
whiting out all the pink

you want to help me ease

into the deep
from dusk to dawn

you tell me not to fear
my fear

to mock the malignant tumors
that grow like night-blooming datura

until they open into moonflowers

you say fighting the darkness
will only tighten the noose

but it is a brutal loop

without end

the days die
and i clutch at the edges of twilight

awaiting your roguish rap
on my window

when you'll come to steal me away
on your pirate ship of clouds

      my long-awaited Thief

and we will sail through the black
together

because the only way out

is on the other side
of night

after the wedding (Designing woman)

for Peggy

in a pink clouded dress of Givenchy's softest tulle

perfectly smudged red
with bright Chanel lipstick

smartly scented
with Blooming Gucci perfume

     and name-dropping like a Boss

i titillate with my giggle
                      (liberated from mothballs for the occasion)
two tuxedos
     Armani is bearded
     Brioni, clean-shaven

and my petite feet
     fitted in bubbly
     Louboutins

flirt

with Ferragamo oxfords that stand
beneath black
tailored trousers

lilting lithely like lovebirds
my champagne slippers delight

in easily eluding the oxfords

(not *too* much
but just enough)

as we play false
a game of hide-and-seek

brown tendrils escape
a tender french twist

and my laughter takes my breath away

i stumble across a dumbwaiter

and scramble in

about to let loose the rope
ready for the ride
of a lifetime
      (or at least
      the ride of the nighttime)

when i see Armani and Brioni
closing in

      my reflection glints in their perfect white teeth
      and in their smiling liquid eyes

i almost hear them thinking

      she's our kill
      of the night

so i grin girlishly

relinquish the rope

throw my arms up in glee

and plunge downwards

eyes open

lips lisping out a piercing whistle

      soon a fullblown howl

when i peek back up above

my two charming tuxedos are bemused
their arms empty

save for one lone Louboutin in Armani's left hand
and scraps of torn Givenchy tulle in Brioni's right

perfectly smeared
with red Chanel lipstick

cut to the quick

i.

you cut to the quick
distracted

unobserved rivulets
run red
blood

drip

drip

drips
from the tips of your fingers

accidental torturer
needles under your nails
sometimes
you push too deep

ii.

the film cuts to black

the reel ends
while the screen goes

dark

dark

darker

as though the dark were always there
                    beneath
moving pictures

as though the black
        wait
                wait
                        waits
for light to imprint an image

        AnythingAnythingAnything

so it knows
                Finally
what to be

iii.

you cut slowly to the green wick
sheltered behind
birch rind

the tree's living skin
thin smooth waxy
too easily scraped by dirty fingernails

no longer green when stripped
from its tender heartwood

don't cut too close to the quick

everything bleeds

Methuselah, Medusa, and Me

I. Methuselah

Tenacious greys hide
among the light brown locks
of my youth

Wiry and unrepentant,
removable only with pliers
rather than tweezers

the greys sprout from my scalp

like bent paper clips
scattered throughout a pile of straw

Have I been touched by ageless Methuselah
too soon?

At thirty-one, has he come for me?
Has he come to save an early sinner from
drowning in floods of
righteous submission
       like those his grandson Noah
       skimmed across so easily
       on his wooden surfboard?

Perhaps old Methuselah can see
the boiling seas rising, coming for us all
while we turn our eyes
       away from the tsunamis
       away from the earth
       towards heaven's gates

with the same passive reverence
that led Noah to forget
the unicorns, the jackelopes

those oddballs
who couldn't surf
and died out too soon

in Jehovah's scalding tempest

Methuselah stroked the head
of my child aunt
Marilyn

Dead by sixteen
        and fully grey,
saved from the reality God had planned for her
alive but lifeless
        in an iron lung
trapped in the limbo He fashioned
for her from polio,
        His latest plague
        during the 1950s

With her soft grey hair
        was Marilyn taken or spared?

II. Medusa

Perhaps age is simply
spinning my hair into silver;
maybe the wiry silver strands
will twist to wily silver serpents
spawn of Medusa herself
as she watches me
unaware

       each of us alone
       on either side of my mirror

Perhaps I will wake one day soon
       my pillow covered in sleepy snakelets
some still snoring peacefully
       little littermates
piled together on top of my head
others curled gently by my face
       softly hissing as they flicker my cheeks
       affectionately
       with their forked tongues

Slew too soon, alone
       with no one to look her in the eyes

Medusa still laughs gently
       through my mirror
at the sight of a poor poetess
grappling with her greys and trochees
       mouth and eyes gaping
       at their sudden plenty

from drinking at her son
Pegasus' well

Charmed by her distant clouded chuckle
I close my eyes
        focus intently on the sound
        as it grows cheerful as a harness bell

Able to bear it no longer,
I need to know
the face that can giggle so
        as though still a young girl

As I bring my curious eyes to the mirror
look directly into Medusa's gaze

I see that she laughs and is beautiful

petting her hair
of wild silver serpents
as she watches me
        in turn

cautiously bring a hand up
to my own greying mane

and feel the caress of her gift
        not deadly
        but rather full of life

a tangle of baby snakes

who shiver in pleasure
as I stroke them gratefully

Humility

for A

When he laughs with me,
I am humbled.

When he tells me
I have a good heart

and I know he believes it,
I am humbled.

When I hold him in this heart
that he believes is good

and I feel myself held
in his gentle glow,

I am humbled.
When I see that he doesn't carry,

he disarms me too, like a shotgun,
until I can't remember where

my bullets ever were.

Mixed-Media Collage

The path is made of broken glass
I start to walk
                    I'm painstaking
The shards puncture my soles
And I start to bleed

I remember my pretty Silver Slippers
Suddenly I'm holding them
So I ease them onto my sobbing feet
And watch the blood seep into the fabric
Staining my pretty silver slippers Ruby Red

I start to walk again
                    Slowly slowly
There has to be more than this

Crosses my mind
The path becomes Yellow Brick
Cheerful and chalky with yellow dust
That sticks to my wet silver-red slippers
Like thick pollen for fat bumblebees

I watch my feet
                    Prancing now
A fleeting smile passes my lips
I see that the precious shoes
Cling to the yellow dust
                    Just as the dust clings to the shoes
Now they're the color of bright buttery sunlight

I start to hum
          I'll take the high road you'll take the low road
                    And I'll be in Scotland before ye

But this Yellow Road is neither
High nor low
Rather a middle path which doesn't end
On the bonny banks of Loch Lomond
    At least not yet

A pocket watch appears in my hand
As I remember
The very important date
  For which I'm running late
    (I'm late I'm late I'm late)

It's a secret but
I'm planting a garden for someone
And it's time to tend

The Yellow Road lets me veer off to where
My garden lies in a sunny glade I found
One day long ago
  Hiding inside my ribcage
And slowly I learned to nurture it
Wanted it to survive outside the protective circle
  Of my body too

I remove my pretty yellow slippers and walk
Bare feet tender but healing
Into the tall grass

Milkweed grows high and the purple clover
    They've been here all along
With the orange monarchs
  (So many newborns)

And fuzzy bumblebees
Drinking juicy nectar

I see the trellis where I planted morning glories
And moonflowers

    (Something will always grow if there's light)
The glories are bright as the noonday sky
And the royal purple pansies look at me
Innocent and joyful and just a little haughty

My vegetable patch is still growing
The cherry tomatoes not yet ripe
I imagine the day they will be sweet and humid

I will smile so my dimples show deep
And feed one to you
Watch as your eyes flutter closed for a delicious moment
Then let you feed me one too

It's okay that you're not ready yet
Things are as they need to be

And one day it will rain

For now, I probe the inner layers of my Self
Full as they are with mixed metaphors
Covered with quilts of Giddy Fairytales
       Wayward Folksongs
            And Consecrated Fables
Stitched by my grandmother
Upcycled by my mother
And torn apart and regenerated by me in collage

I line its edges with a mosaic of broken glass
       It must be crossed to enter the picture
Inside are fabrics of shiny Silver Satin
       Red Jacquard with Ruby Sequins
          Soft Yellow Pashmina
             Stitched onto the canvas

For extra texture I add
A patch of shorn fur from a boastful white rabbit
       Who has one eye always on his pocket watch
          The other on the finish line
And an ancient tortoise who lives in my garden
       Gave me a piece of her oracle shell
          That can be divined

Finally there is the garden
With green cotton milkweed
Embroidered purple pansies and clover
Painted blue acrylic morning glories
Terrycloth bumblebees
Delicate monarch butterflies
       Cut from tissue paper and
       Washed orange with watercolors

I leave room to grow

Duration

I am a small volcano
outside, beyond your front window

or perhaps a musket
that cannot trust God
to keep its powder dry.

I ask, Can you trust me
not to destroy the things I love?

I ask, Can we trust the morning
not to steal the evening star?

Yes, you say,
your eruption is just a car backfiring
outside, beyond the front window.

Yes, you say,
the morning steals away the night
but she leaves the evening star in her back pocket,
           like an Ace that she plays
           when dusk falls.

Rites of Passage

the florist cuts the lilies
and the lilies bleed

she sloughs the blood off
into a bucket

and tosses the lilies into the river

(purity is meat at the slaughterhouse)

before the violinist callouses
he blisters
and the blisters break
and his fingers bleed

he ignores them
keeps playing a sound that tastes
like silver

and a red river runs through the f-holes
where nothing used to be

Post-Modern Papyrus

When everything is new, or maybe old
but newly remembered by my heartbeat—

that's when I lose all use for language.

Every word is a platitude in the face
of something entirely new,
and so I fear the naming of unknown things.
If mere observation inherently changes
the observed, what must become lost
within the chalk body-outline
of irrevocable classification?

Regrettably unaware of its uselessness,
my verbose voice box chatters
in a fluid string of toneless, banal syllables
as I lead it, oblivious, onto a raft
pushing it away from shore,
sending it down the river and through the reeds
like Moses.

Out of sight, the hollow soliloquy fades to silence.
Distracted, I estimate how long it will be before
my little chatterbox is found
spouting platitudes among the swampy reeds
and hailed by the inarticulate as a prophet of rare insight.

Absent-minded, I make a mental note
to expect guerrilla proselytizers armed
with glossy pamphlets printed
on non-recyclable paper, advertising
"The All-New, Tax-Exempt 501(c)(3) Non-Profit
Church of the Divinely-Endowed Voice Box"

      (or whatever)
sometime within the next six months or so.

But no matter now.
Everyday objects around me blur
into an impressionistic mess of light
and texture. Words and names
fall away as colors bleed
through me quickly like watercolors
through tissue paper.

Wet and pulpy, I drop
clumps of the sopping paper
(which sobs pathetic rainbow tears
as it nears cellular breakdown)
into my blender, wincing as the blade
rips the sodden stuff to mush.

I spread and flatten the pulp with a rolling pin,
bake it until it's dry
and stiff and thick
and brittle.

Hot homemade papyrus, straight from the oven—
      just like the ancient Egyptians used to make,

only probably rougher and bumpier
and overall much more difficult to write on.

There will never be a clean slate.

Words can be lost
          abandoned
          rejected
          recanted

but not erased.

So now I recycle my names and words
for things and record patched-together
insights on my ever-improving
homemade batches
of post-modern papyrus.

Because nothing in this world is ever entirely new

except,
perhaps,
for our understanding.

Indifferent Prose

Love must surely be the most-chosen and most-intimate and most-dear theme of mostly-poets. Mostly-poets mostly write poems, and those poems are mostly love poems. These mostly-poets grow their strings of loving words into strands of connective tissue, linked together by the merging of ink and page. Insensibly sensitive to the sentient succinctness that commands our surrender to feeling—to love—the mostly-poets try to trap any remaining woven strands of tissue and cage them on the page between parallel lines.

The strands unweave at their own leisure, forgotten in the sweaty fever of the moment that breaks, inevitably, sometime in the night while their creators sleep and dream of a vase they bought together at a summer street festival, surrounded by sunflowers, and how the vase was broken that night in the sweaty heat of a moment that passed too quickly to recall clearly. But when they awoke in the green of morning, the vase was in pieces next to them on the tiled kitchen floor.

In this next paragraph, my thesis will be that the opposite of Love is not Hate; rather, the opposite of Love is Indifference. Hate is Love's alter-ego, sprung from heady emotion like Athena, fully grown, from Zeus's forehead—ready to sever Love's skull from its spine. Hate is the villain to Love's hero, and they are pathetically, heartbreakingly co-dependent protagonists—as every mostly-poet worth her salt and sugar will tell you. One cannot exist without the other.

Ah, but Indifference…

Indifference would be the perfect topic for a philosophy exam ("Indifference: Force of Liberation or Destruction? Explain your answer in 25 words or less." Tangential but crucial question: "Does Indifference Exist? Correct answers worth 10 bonus points.").

Indifference would be an excellent scientific experiment. The question: Would Homo sapiens choose Indifference alone over both Love and Hate? The hypothesis: Test subjects' responses will depend on their varied experiences, the emotions those experiences eventually evoked, and the ripeness of the emotions experienced; however, test subjects will overwhelmingly come to the conclusion, while lying alone in the middle of the bed at the edge of night, that they could never choose Indifference over Love, even if Hate were to always tag along on the sidelines in every coupling like the proverbial third wheel. Test subjects will then succumb swiftly to sleep. They will not ask themselves if Indifference exists. They will not question whether Indifference, if it exists, is liberating or destructive. They will not question what it means to be liberated or what it is to be destroyed. It will not occur to them that one test subject's liberation is another's destruction.

Only the mostly-poets will continue to wax and wane their words; to count the pieces of a broken vase and either crumble them into dust or glue them back together into an imperfect ideal. Mostly-poets never need to know Now whether Indifference exists, or not. Their brains and bones have held the answer always.

And for Now, all they can do is capture the moment, before it fades fleetingly like pollen floating in a sunbeam.

About the Author

Liana Kapelke-Dale holds a B.A. in Spanish Language and Literature from the University of Wisconsin-Milwaukee and a J.D. from the University of Wisconsin Law School. Her poetry has been featured most recently in such journals as *Big Easy Review, Fleas on the Dog, Grand Little Things, Impossible Task,* and *The Fabulist,* among others. Liana's first chapbook of poetry, *Specimens,* was published in 2012, and a second haiku chapbook, *Little words seeking/Mute human for mutual/Gain and maybe more,* was published in early 2020. She currently lives in Milwaukee, WI, with her lovely pointer-hound mix, Poet.

www.ingramcontent.com/pod-product-compliance
Lightning Source LLC
Chambersburg PA
CBHW020303090426
42735CB00009B/1199